Salt on the eye

Also by Hanne Bramness

Korrespondanse
I sin tid
Nattens kontinent
Revolusjonselegier
Regnet i Buenos Aires
Salt på øyet

for children:

Kysset
Trollmåne

Also by Frances Presley

The Sex of Art
Hula Hoop
Linocut
Neither the One nor the Other, with Elizabeth James
Automatic cross stitch, with Irma Irsara
Somerset letters
Paravane
Myne – new and selected poems & prose 1975-2006

Hanne Bramness

Salt on the eye
selected poems

translated by
Hanne Bramness & Frances Presley

Shearsman Books
Exeter

First published in in the United Kingdom in 2007 by
Shearsman Books Ltd
58 Velwell Road
Exeter EX4 4LD

www.shearsman.com

ISBN-13 978-1-905700-41-7

ISBN-10 1-905700-41-5

Original poems copyright © Gyldendal Norsk Forlag, 1983, 1986; and copyright © J.W. Cappelens Forlag AS, 1992, 1996, 2002, 2006.
Translations copyright © Hanne Bramness and Frances Presley, 2007.

The right of Hanne Bramness to be identified as the author of this work has been asserted by her in accordance with the Copyrights, Designs and Patents Act of 1988. The rights of Hanne Bramness and Frances Presley to be identified as the translators of this work have also been so asserted. All rights reserved.

Cover illustration, 'Island Sun Two' by Renée DesChamps.
Copyright © Renée DesChamps, 2006.

Acknowledgements

The author and publisher wish to thank Gyldendal Norsk Forlag and J.W. Cappelens Forlag AS for permission to publish these translations. The poems first appeared in the following collections: *Korrespondanse* (1983) and *I sin tid* (1986), both published by Gyldendal Norsk Forlag; *Nattens kontinent* (1992), *Revolusjonselegier* (1996), *Regnet i Buenos Aires* (2002) and *Salt på øyet* (2006), all published by J.W. Cappelens Forlag.

This translation has been published with the financial support of NORLA (Norwegian Literature Abroad).

Contents

Early Poems
Listening to Duncan in the heart of Uppland 10
Twilights 11
Paul Klee pictures 13
Matisse 1952 with a quotation from Rilke 15
Cut up of an early poem 17

from *In her time*
In her time 20
The choice 38
A sceptic's serenade 41
Murder in Uppsala in June 42
Stockholm days 46

from *Night's continent*
Night's continent 52
Castlerigg, a stone circle in the north 62
Wolves are standing in your dream 64

from *Revolution elegies* 65

from *Rain in Buenos Aires* 78

from *Salt on the eye*
Vacuum 94
Passenger 95
Bungalow 96
The moon in Loo's house 97
The admirer 98
Terri's house 99
Halloween 100

"That the juices may flow in them / And the juices lie."	101
Transfer	102
Haunted	103
Soundtrack	104
from Desert conditions	105
In the dark	108
Visible and invisible	109
The bathtub's history	110
The limitless	111
Purification	112
Primitive	113
Knife in the water	114
Loo's memory	115
Real and unreal light	116
A white spot	117
Exposure	118
Passage	119
Florence revisited	120
She has gone before	121
Imprisoned	123
Preserved	124
Creatures	125
Notes	126

Early poems

Listening to Duncan in the heart of Uppland

A return to
this island   these woods
this ancient lake
here
the sentence
if it speaks does it speak in a foreign tongue?
I took this island to be
my meadow
and now the more I speak the more I see it
changed
    – as we look things change
beyond recognition   we read
travel into thought
artistry and seven colours of the rainbow
into flowers
heart beat into clocks
senses
revolve in reading: deep recognition of the lake at night
    calls me – when I call out
this is Linnaeus' landscape
but I can only believe it or know it
so constructed: I pulled up a small tree to get an idea of the roots
Duncan's voice
carves a space in the night like light
the silent notes of the wind
a peace of no certainty
a meadow where the flowers turn   hardly detectable now
beyond this porch

Twilights

I would
    lift up my eyes
   see the evening
sink down into the light
descend on
    words   streets I knew were there
   and grass
    the room high up still warm
from the sunshine
abundant unreachable sun
       lingering still
on birds' wings
over the city

    and Rosa Luxemburg
   for her part
     "would continue standing in the middle of
the street
numbering the stars as they came out"
       lit it would seem
   by the birds
flying higher
   in the warm sky   the depth
  of the eyes
counting reading another day's end
into night-fall
caught
   between following the day's procedure out of habit
  and not wanting its
  inevitable ending
     caught between rest and making
  the moment last
     "unwilling to leave the mild air"

seeing the grocer's boys and other boys running
shouting
    into the disappearing day
"and the twilight"
        that opening
between work and supper and
        carrying the rubbish out
   lovers leaning toward each other
imaging the air
     "in which day and night were so gently
   caressing one another"

Paul Klee pictures

Sketch of a street in a town

The man's fine limbs
black lines
    running from
  bone to muscle
plaster is tendons
      tension in stone

Vor dem Schnee

I have seen the kingdom of
air so stiff
     darken and
the trees
so wild in the wind
          continuous
  one line only
and softer colours
  before the snow
fell

The thirty-six hours before the air is softened by
snow
    An icy lake
    a day
    clear and grey

Pictures look at us from that
painter's workshop
          the park resembles Van Gogh
resembles what we see when we
          look back

Gate of the deserted garden

Turn
    black earth   red earth
    learn to love
          a human animal vegetable world
with the uproar of
    death

Matisse 1952 with a quotation from Rilke

From all sides
the figure is one-dimensional
blue
ornamental

like a pressed flower
in a sketch book

*The painful operation has
made me into a philosopher*

cut directly into the colours
one motion
definitive

The hotel
a metaphor for nature
the room with a view
a filter for light

*I will render my feelings
things around me create them in me*

The blue arm
with the hand behind the neck

like half a peach
with a stone

The Mediterranean
the strong clear colours

rude and repulsive colour

*my dear wife you are the
lucky victim of a portrait*

The thread to the Greek
urn motif

humans caught in a life ring
faint as plants
wild as animals

Die geheimnisvolle Worte...
a coat-of-arms for joy

the blue figure
bends into the text
and reads of its beginning

Cut-up of an early poem

This night
spring
you
were born
severed
that darkness
you rose
a star trailed
first lights
broke into your lungs
found voice
numbers return
place
a year
the dwelling
threatened
half-remembered coast
this dawn
layer on this night
constellations of air
tracts
the underground river
note its waters nor remember
river persists
continued sound
descend
a refuge
nor anything like water
hearts frozen
restored by the sun
currents
day lost
passages

receding waters
to touch
a beginning

from
In her time

Whisper an order
to the future: in her time
draw lines
        across lines
and speak:

Of the midsummer night
                  a journey east
    the horizon
           pushed foward
with the boat
        dead calm
and in the water the boat lights' pillars
    stand firm

           somewhere
we cross the line
                between east and west
north of the 60th parallel
    at the time
            when night turns
and earth tilts its axis
    unnoticeably toward
                the sun

*"The first flight of man, outside of dream,
seen as stone and stainless steel —"*

Of her
    a woman standing
   on a western beach
thinking of flight
        the brothers Wright

here
    at Kitty Hawk
        pale sands shift continuously
their line in the waters
       broken by waves
  The sea comes towards me across the sea

– their courage
   who stepped out of dreams
          took to their wings
from their dreams
   into the wind

they counted
      59 seconds in the air
  the world was no longer the same

Of her
   standing
in the shadow of the monument
         a wing stranded
  of steel and stone
      thinking
of the "ocean" that separates
  this shadow from the dawn of the century

Of the oceans
   when the whales signalled
to each other
         between poles
  wandering along
            magnetic lines

– we do not know
   before we interrupt

uninterrupted and unique: nature
  navigates

Of the beach
       the sands
  the line that the wind
shifts
    and the ocean

Of him
>   Thomas Hariot
>   on his westward journey
>   who measured the star's height
on the earth a point
>   imagined
> and coordinated
>   for the movement of body and boat:
>   *answerable to the surge of the sea*
to find a path
  on that limitless plain
he read
    cosmos into the nights
  the days

he
  a figure in the bow head
  north of the 20th parallel
holds his clock toward the sun
>   and the compass
  he is
    outside his dream and out
on the ocean

Paths are
   paths of thought
  human paths in air
      and on the ocean
  that in its depths hides
       the past
or dreams

we do not know
  maybe the Azores or Thera
        are the peaks of Atlantis
because most dreams
      are memories or possibilities
  we are the carriers of

"The sea" is also
     Debussy's dream
by the instrument

La musique souvent me prend comme une mer!

there
  at the limit of words
and in the gaps between notes
       is a silence
  which does not silence

Of words
      these
   prisons of things
"on the one side of the ocean
and the other"

he reads his dream
                  into the instrument
   and notes answer him
in the same instant

words
   stories that
spin times into *one* thread

in the same interval
                  the sun rises
as night falls

Along
      latitudes
they measured the sun's height
                take soundings

    if I draw a line
between traces in time from
Pisa to
      Petrograd
      – Galileo who saw the lamp
      measured and recognized the oscillations
      in the blood

to this pendulum
    that swings in the Isaac cathedral
that with gravity is moved by earth: shows
    earth's movement

I see
      science and religion
    side by side

What
       do I see in this city
    in the east
            other than what I know

where is the entrance?

reflections on
         what I see become
   a reflection of that
I have seen

where in the world is what is new!

I see
   decay
    in the shadow of the golden domes
                          great ones!
   the dark *eternal fire*
in sharp sunlight
and pollen
       along sidewalks
and on sunburnt lawns
  see
      Andrei Rublev painting
this summer snow on the sky
   the transparent sky
              at night
the city sinks into its deep
                and in the river
the city is always new
like Kitezh
       preserved by legend

Of decay
        a promise of change
decayed
        into legend

Kitezanka finds her way home
                            through rain
and bullets
        to her city because
  it is outside of time
                outside
the true twentieth century
  (a dream has come
                true)

here
    in time / in this place /
    – is it so? have promises been lured by
amor fati
        love of a fate
that enamoured declares:
    evil shall drive away evil
    fear shall clear the blood

This century of peace treaties
   in the sign of the passport
      new maps are being drawn
      new lines set

for the sake of what world?
                        do people break up
   from their homes
            in strange lands
set out on a journey
              away from history
   that is rewritten
laws are adjusted

on their way back nothing
awaits them: sun in panes of windows
   in houses built
            on oblivion's firm ground

Of balance
    and in the borderlands of
a balanced world picture: prisons

If I draw a line
    south
            – meeting the flock of migrating birds
in spring
along 30 degrees east
                    over the black earth
crossing the rivers
south
      to Istanbul and further east
    to the country wiped off the map

in Kurdistan
    the calendar disintegrates
the new year
          flames in the vernal equinox
    and in the prisons
               death confirms
only its own
time

On the road
    along the river: Voronezh
  by Don
    the river breaking into the picture
of spring in the east

– he who sits
    bent over his papers
  listening through the night
hearing wind closing doors
  faint water on his breath
      the heart's pace
in the room
suffering fright's strength
     / the strong tea
    the strong cigarettes /

What happens
    to the body
  in exile
submitted to its own deadline
for thought
    what happens to language
in constant opposition
  to the laws?

    They sink
down into their own premonitions
  write their own fall

Also by drifting snow
    over dark woods
                      light above holes in the ice
we interpret "spring"
in the north

        time follows the wind
                  following
longitudes
      ranges of hills: *Spring*
which should not be measured by the calendar
but by the climate and the warmth

    where in the year
are the seasons' limits?
                by the Nile
birds rise
    Sirius visible only *one* morning
in the belt of dawn

Time in the stars: another time
        in the riverbed
                water
the salt ocean
        in the cell
    that continues its life in the tissue
another time in the blood
               than in the mind

in "the great wheel": the axis
        runs through the heart
               a face
can be detected in the clocks
when times are coordinated
                they disappear

poems
      stories
disappear

Of her
    who writes
from prison
    of spring
    the only thing that will never tire her
reads biology
      poetry

Wenn nicht mehr Zahlen und Figuren
Sind Schlüssel aller Kreaturen

in the forgotten Gothic script of Novalis
another order

      hears the twitter
  at dusk
      the hour between day and night
pushed forward
      in time
drawing a line
      from one spring
  to another
      from Warsaw to Wronke to Breslau:
prisons
    that reign over a darkness
  birds will not obey

Time in the stars: other times
   in water
         in its currents
and undertows: in autumn
               the chill towards the bottom
where sun does not reach
          the skin
   and in the eyes
       the light

the late clear afternoons
   when the sky is in the water
              the flock of migrating
birds blacken its surface

pictures pressing against the skin
   the eye
       meeting resistance
in thought: *the sloughs and sluices*
of my mind

Of the birds
              their flight
above woods
              cities
   crossing latitudes
                     rivers
the winds' wake
                the blue Mediterranean
   following their time
                   under the sun
held up by a resistance
     Leonardo saw
                in the air

but
    the movable wings
   did not bring him closer to
flight
art never copies:

   when a man dancing catches his prey
he follows his own rhythm

"Walking the world, through the people at airports, this city of hills, this island ocean fire blue and now this city"

    Now
            in this city times
    standing
            side by side

   are *now*
            the Winter Palace
   the Summer Garden
    sun's play
   in the afternoon
               the wind's shadows
    on the canal
   on the stone wall
               green seaweed from
    high tide

        all is here
   in view
        clearly
     enlarged

The choice

> *A burst*
> *of confidence. Confiding*
>
> *a treasured thing*
>
> *kept inside,*
> *as if it were a burden*

I know
    house and roof
do not feel the rain

the tree has no memory
        only when it falls
  are its years numbered
        in the split stone's kernel
        is stone

water does not dance!

the bird does not sing in the poem

the country is not untouched

I see
under the cloud's tower
a furrowed line
        a medieval horizon
hills forced by plough
   and harrow

a history of tools
        I see

through   my fingers   see
through language

the power is not the wind

kings die like saints do
   blood spilled
   – they are forgotten in their gold

the insight
the fire
     that gave the Celts their iron
   was their baptism

but I know
the power is not
the gods
borders are shifted
backwards and forwards
         in four continents I saw
         no map was a mirror
   in Persia
     on the line between hemispheres
I saw them divorce
      father from daughter
   and son
what could I do?

the other one
     the initiated
he who sees the orbits of stars
         who interprets birds' song

who knows ecstasy
          who hears the magic of the spheres
he
advises kings   holds a key in his hands

but it is not the bird
that sings in the poem!

the movement of time cannot be read
in numbers alone

I know this and I have chosen
                says the poet
but how do I live with a choice
   as if it was fated?

A sceptic's serenade

Does the hot earth hold close
to its face its lips words
does the red tree in the heart
of fruits hold a darkness
in the shadow of leaves
do the sands of the desert
hold a late light from stars
in white granules and
does the open pool in
the earth hold a sun
is there an echo of deep strokes
from huge clocks rising
in the night over fields
and the harbour with shoals
of stars and a green moon
do upturned longing eyes
correspond with a writing
in strange bodies
does the will wrestle in the marrow
with heat from the brown earth
and blue shadows in the blood
with ice

Murder in Uppsala in June

1

Time
was it a clock
that struck?

four dark eyes
and twelve strokes

we are together but
still alone
here

each in our time
imprisoned
by the stories
from our lives

you speak
and you are back in a mosque
where you chanted for
a dead conquerer
in his language

you a stranger
in a strange land

2

The murderer
was also a stranger

on a different street
in this same town
a Kurd
a Turkish informer
is killed by a Kurd from France

a strange darkness
in his shadow
that made his way through the crowd

he was caught without
a comprehensive explanation
as expected

3

Strangers
and in the name of war
the death of strangers becomes
a motion

rolling! there is
no turning back

twenty thousand deported
is a necessity

like the flight of swallows
or the migration of whales

turns! rolling over
mountains of sand

forces a path through dark forests
drives on
onwards

4

How shall we
speak our history?

– I hear her voice

when the news that reaches us is
the statistics of strangers

need is no alibi
it is the nature
we live by

but the papers write of terrorists

– I see her dark eyes

5

We must love the sources
of the knowledge we chose

we have no choice

we must attend to
the words

not pure ideas
geometrical experiments lines
drawn on a map:

I write to you my friend
from Qamishli
...
time here is a car
driven by the police

Stockholm days

From this plane
to the stars

city of night's darkness
in frozen silence

how
shall I enter?

it is never quiet
or completely dark

seen from the outside
from the island
by the bridge

Morning comes
a pale sun's pattern
on the glass
lights through the window's frost

the city rises

The city rises

smoke from ice holes
swans on heavy wings

a January day lifts
from the fjord in front of us

I note:
the eye does not see
where change takes place

I read history
into the stones
of the Old Town

buildings painted
new strokes of
red blue yellow
the colours were all baroque

in the
falling snow

City that rises
in snow that falls

two speeds of time touch
their histories

Now
earth tilts its axis
from the sun so that
early afternoon
the day turns
light fades
over bridges and under
sleeping birds float by
on ice floes

The eye sees
its harmony with
those pictures of its time

one that shows
a city rising
1535
when distant orbits of stars
were inscribed
on the Stockholm sky

a landscape
half covered by water

A city that rises
in the snow that falls
nights that halve
the days

I note:

for the eye
the horizon's limit
is always the same

from
Night's continent

Night's continent

The one awake does not see the entrance
into night, a break in
the story, a star
the star in breath, in sleep, just
beyond reach

You showed me oblivion
you rowed the boat into the backlight
over the fjord, you steered
the wind free of the wood through the night
you steered the rain, you wiped
the rain out

The one awake does not see
the rain
against a grey-white wall
half asleep
the morning is a pillar
in foreign water
a sea of outsailed
dreams

The rain begins on the skyline
dies out in mid-air
it narrows in the field of vision
to ashes, a horizon of
ashes

This is the summer with parting
in the wind
I am the wind I meet
inheritor of a parting without end
in the sign of a choice
I carry a burden of
parting, as though I carried
another's child

Way back, in the house
the sun buried
childhood's black dragon by heaven's gate
a promise of
parting

The one awake does not see the entrance into night
light from the star of change shines
too late

torn up, encapsulated in a time
outside dreams
see, night is a thought!

the one awake blinded by memory
does not see the night, but
sees all in blind repetition

You shall forget parting, parting's
shadow! you can let go
into darkness, you can
feed on oblivion

On the approach to landing when
clouds give way to sight of ground
a pause before
the sight reaches the eye, points of time
snow into the dark

You showed me oblivion, showed me
the grey fjord, the grey ice
near the shore, bathed in
a weak sunlight
what I have forgotten is an inverted sun
that glows

I see your mouth on night's
ground, see the words
rise

I see you coming from the mountain down to
the stones on the shore
I see you coming from the nights
you wipe the nights out
you hold the new born child in your arms
before it is born

II

The one awake watching a child
does not see
the child, the one awake does not see
the day, but time
passed, the one awake in remorse
is blinded by its
blessing

Nothing is
more impossible for the sleepless
than the impossible, no change, no
forgiving
occurs

The one awake sees
the watchful eye, you see it in the one
you love

We were taught
will, that will should rule, but
the will does not sleep
it dances for the watchful eye
self-sacrificing
wide awake

We were taught submission, nor is submission
sleep, but a strict
hierarchy, a stern lover
the next generation
and the next, born of a strict
memory

The one awake sees night's
shadow
not night, but the shadow has blood
of ice, dead visions
a strict life

I see
the shadow, bow to
a false baptism
that will initiate me into the circle of the
unaffected, deep inside blind vigilance
I fear for the child, I see only
what is possible

The milk is nothing, nor
the child
the newly born gaze, black as night, a light

a flash of nothing
you, your mouth, are
nothing

Not the night, but the shadow, forces
a confession, that is not why
they sacrificed
to steer the sun's journey across
night's continent

III

The one awake does not see the unborn
child, the seed finds the egg's mouth
on its own
the child lies in the shape of a lion
guarding its tears

The entrance into night is in
the fall, the one that halts in the fall
to see
shall see only himself repeated in the mirror
feel the mirror's ice
in the blood

The one awake sees all as in
a mirror
the horizons are crowded together in a mirror
the size of a
child's head, all is
night, all is a senseless parasite in
the heart

I carry a burden of
blindness
as if I carried a penalty in my womb
beyond redemption
if you only stay awake
sleep's formula will be revealed
if you stay awake long enough
you will give birth to
yourself

By night's limit stands a wall
of protection
a wall of rain protects the rain
the child in the womb
feeds on that blindness, blind snow
blind sleep

I carry a burden of blindness
a sight dead to visions
but the bird you pulled from my lips

escapes
the milk lifts its faceless
stream

IV

What I have forgotten is the night
a river under earth
an opening into another mind
the promise of simultaneous time
what I have forgotten is the rain
that rains
that follows me
down

Initiated by the rain into night's order
deserted on a shore
by morning

The one awake watching over a parting
does not see its space
that sorrow has its star
voices burnt into the mountain
call
high frequency vibrations strike sparks
ignite the shadows

the wind slakes the waking eye
that does not see

The sun disappeared
for an hour the moon shone in sun's autumn
the child slept
the wind began to blow, lifted
the day from the earth

Frozen fast in moon's disc, a speck
on the retina, pressed into a line
of night, held back

the one awake does not see the sun
disappear
but it does, sinking behind
stiff shadows

Where have I been?
the child has passed through me, I was out
brought back by the clock in the delivery room
the first, naked gaze
did I see it?
caught in a dream, surrendered to the star
in breath
once long ago
birth occurs

What I have forgotten is the beginning
I carry a burden of sleep to protect against
the possible, that is why
they sacrificed, in surrender, bowed in
towards their own beginnings

The wind that chases the shadows
lifts the day
the plane that races its engines
sends shudders of pain to the spine
with the speed of darkness

You showed me oblivion, you breathed
a light into me, a sun
you breathed skin onto shadows
I fall in your light
rivers under the earth
rivers in a maze under the city
rise and sink

I ask you for everything, but
all is yours
the boat you rowed, the child you gave
the wind, promises you left behind
in the hangar
I have seen you before, I have noticed
your nakedness

Castlerigg, a stone circle in the north

From the mountains the rain
comes
in concentric circles
sailing, hiding the eye of
the sun

The stones in the sun
circle in
the day, but rain wipes out
the shadows

For the eye blinded by
sight, stones are as airy
as rain
as invisible as their shadow
in rain

Deep is the rain, deeper
than rivers
under the earth, that rise, than
the child in the womb

In the open wind the year
drowns

The sky tall
as a timeless
tower
Rain falls
through
midsummer nights
with sun
rainy days
winter moons

The year drowns
in the rain
years drown
but the stones glow
in the shadow of time's
circle

It is the same
rain
the same sail from
the mountains

Wolves are standing in your dream

Out in the rain, out in the snow
They come with the spring night's winds
that breathe on the window
in the dawn
They come with the migrating birds
hatch when love's struggle
has taken place, give birth
through their mouths
They embrace your naked body
living shadows of frost

from

Revolution elegies

Behind your curtain, word, the rain is shut
out, and the eye must give way to your
clear-sightedness

there was a battle over the story, over sun
and moon, which freed the shadows
of a soul

now dreams float in a sphere of dreams and
the rain has returned
to its own

The rain stops at the window, streets
rise in the day like worms in the rain
all to one level: surveyable

the word has torn out the rain's heart
what is dead is lost now
the invisible is invisible

This is not morning's domain, it takes a while
to lift us into light, close the door to the night
behind us, timber the floor with props

it takes a while before the landscape will settle
trees that bristled resisting with their roots
in the air

– it takes time to lift them into place, floating
unruly time, the word covers, smoothes over, erases
a crack

the word splits us, plunges a part of us back into
dreams, before it pulls us up, makes us
stand

– still trembling, it takes a while before the day
is twisted into shape and light has filled all
chinks and hollows

– burned the moon ash pale, we approach the window
sense that the moon is our own image, a mirror
far off

It takes a while to get size, distances into order
and soften the blood's voice that speaks so loudly
of running time

that it threatens to drown the sensible word
but only a while, the moment it takes to gather
time together, lay it dead

and draw a divide, empty us, make us into
what we can understand and control, and so
control us

Have we begun to speak? The word tears us out of
morning, lands us in a darkness that we think is light
it is a tunnel

– why do we push the child down the tunnel
of time until it starts running to
catch up?

If we steer, hold on so tight that the knuckles
whiten, will we then make it, manage to lift
from ourselves

will we be able to put confusion behind us
can we achieve such speed that we are released from
the wasted circles of thought

will we be able to drive past the heart's call
tear away, so that we finally rise into a sphere
of sorrow?

It must have taken time to make us accept
calm, a sail in calm waters under
the stars, under the same sun
day after day

so that we pay no attention to the gusts of wind
but believe we are wrong, believe that tears
that catch up with us are a fault
and that we are bewildered

when we feel the transparency, when I for
a moment do not know whether I am mother or
child, whether my hand is big or small, if I can
can be distinguished from snow

Hold my head in your hands, a light
streams from your fingers, a wave runs through
me, I become transparent

– in your grip, all shadows of who I was
all the mouths I had, you gather in your hands
hold on tight

When you walk to the window you have already
forgotten that you were out, the wind
inside of you drops

the ski-track meets the ski-track, touches
the slope in passage, the eye forces
the day down where it was

as if nothing happens; thoughts awakened
pull a protecting curtain of forgetfulness
across the eye

In the midst of the hot noise there is
an unpeopled place, a cool flight
you must fear

Even when the sun beckons with heat
on the sill, brushes your lips, pushes
through with its slight beams

feeds your mouth that thirsts after
light, when it turns you around and reshapes
you, you are still snow refusing to melt

you keep standing steadfast gazing at
the icicle under the eaves
pulling yourself forward

Even when the rain rushes over the woods
dead snow runs into the earth, winter's
light ebbs, you hold back

you ride no wave of rain, but pull
away holding on to abstract reins, pushing
your forehead against the pane

Stiffened fingers, stiff from water, white from
wind, a carton home, softened paper, here rests
a cheek

verily I say unto you, he who cannot
lift himself above litter, is as good as
not born

The returning child, you see its slender
back by the window, wants to make sure
the cars bring dusk ashore

tiptoeing into the dark to check whether the moon
hangs in place, if it has fastened
its shadows to earth

all constantly threatening to disintegrate!
– distances covered without your
presence, you are a figure

mistakenly identical to yourself, only slighter
like a child, perfectly grateful for
stagnation

Where does tenderness come from, it reshapes
the lips, they fold out, it swallows and
swallows in me at the sight of you, drawing
from me like cool water

where does tenderness come from that offers such
resistance! – the head bursting from the
inside, the tongue entering the tongue, prepared
to let go

You look up, see the moon in its castle, a moment
it swings like a pendulum, makes the chest
chime

as in a picture you noticed; the moon is
pregnant, a moment you are pregnant with the moon, you
glow, stagger

the moon dipped in your gaze, the head swirls, but there is a
weight you recognize, a form
falling into place

Snow takes you home, when it snows you see
double, an image of snow stuck to the retina
comes through

it dances in your gaze, limping, but
confident, it is a snowfall stored in memory
a familiar cold

a place you come from, all the windows you
gazed out of and saw the whirling movement and
the darkness behind

Milk has frozen in the glasses, over the table top
shines a blue light, the rest is
in the dark

here I can touch a membrane of darkness, burn myself on
a glass, the blue light crackles in my eye
when the perspective is shifted

Tenderness strikes – time does not stand
still, catches up with us, returns to
find us, we encounter it

– in an undressed gaze, in the sight of a
tablecloth waving, surrendered to slow
wind, not in keeping with its own beat

on my way down via Appia Nouva – a stab
of darkness in the crowded light, suddenly
pushed out

There is a way from the neck and
down, running along the spine, a column
of seed, where grains of thought lie
glowing

We are familiar with an opposing light, have
seen it through cracks along seams
in the cranium

Rain in Buenos Aires

Time that lifts scabs off wounds, lets
them sift down like snow, brushes
against the ventricle echo chambers – a dark
note, an answer – time that is islands in the blood,
currents and cool mud, the motion of silt
in spiralling water.

Time that opens up a snowy morning
(the view of ankle-deep snow between
ageing buildings), forced wide open
then tightened, drives a wedge in,
floods the hollows with pale sunlight, striking
a note that reverberates in the voice.

Beyond a condition of time that is
constant, there is still the rain in Buenos
Aires, a fine drizzle left hanging
in the air above a courtyard, giving
the blind man back his sight, opening the black
gaze of a rose, transforming itself into
yesterday's rain, dying out in a light,
a relief.

Time, genetic babble, a pain
without address. Here with a view of
an asphalt path between great trees, glassy
from thaw, outdated frost;

time, a babbling god, the voice dying in
us, subsiding. A distant gate latched
shut, incomprehensibly.

Time, stranger in a strange room, a
grin the way a child in the end grins from
being beaten, time like a knife's edge,
a dead horizon. A small, round face
behind a window in the house when the night is
clear; time that drops by, turns around
and is gone.

Time nestling a space for mothers, a
break one morning behind the garage, an
autumn sun lighting up white breath. They were
intoxicated, sank down in a pain without
shelter looking over their shoulders, for one
moment leaning back against the raw, quiet
motion of time.

The eye staring at the snowy weather has
lost its memory of snow, flakes
burned onto the retina. It cannot see
how snow makes the lawns float
and melts the paths into dark mirrors.
It does not see spring in the drift, cannot
see an end to it!

Force, a child of order, that
returns, can be almost like a song
to one who doesn't remember anything else, who knows
and doesn't know that a smile must be bent, wrung
into place. Force accompanies the blood, in homeless currents
of plasma *pain islands* are formed, a
buzz in the head.

Force, confidential – warm as weeping, as
porridge, brings comfort like a mother's hand,
yet mother is afraid. It can seem so nice,
but it takes just a small twist,
a small step outside the burning
circle before fear drills small holes in
the brow.

Wistfulness living in the woods around, outside
the house, through cracked walls it oozes
in, at night, the house glows with a sad metallic
glow in this wind. Night after night, it strokes
their waiting watchful cheeks, and they
oblige.

The hand with blue veins that rows away
at dawn (late in the day since autumn is coming
to a close). A hand for-
saken, lost, it has let go of its grip –

sheets flutter like leaves on the wind – the grip is
ever more powerless, ever weaker, but also
kind.

A place on the path through the woods, past the blue
shining comfrey against a yellow wall –
an afternoon the air stood still between
trees – marching slowly with a pram.
In the place where the sun caught the child's wrath of
woollen hair, transitions were
wiped out.

Steaming cars by a garage on a dark
autumn morning, headlamps light up a
crowd of yellow trees, brushing over the slanting
roof with sudden flickers. The voices heard then
crying out their airy messages into that early
hour, are not dead, but distorted
by wind from the stars.

Silence shields the flame. Outside the
light beam – as far as the flame
reaches – it is pitch dark. If you walk
fast darkness will grow, if you slow
down the light increases, shines. Thus stillness
reveals your limits, while restlessness
will make you blind.

A deep cut in the night for light, just
on the night-line; to make lips, a mouth
in the skin of night where light can shine forth,
a wound, a star-wound in the soft cupola
of night, points that define
darkness surrounding.

Water-darkness under the membrane of night –
like a river pushed up under thin
ice – it glides in us, past us, its breath
speaks in the still air.

Rain rushing mild over Buenos
Aires, turns on its vertical axis
and drives through the horizon, falling
in San Telmo, Recoleta, Palermo and across
the suburbs that no longer exist. A few
cars approach, drive back through
death, coming almost within reach then
turn back, because the afternoon
grows lighter.

Unsteady floors in a home that slant
and slope this way and that,
a cupboard comes sliding, doors
flutter, glasses fall off shelves,

as randomly as rain. Behind hazy
windows, the shadows of figures that
hold on tight.

This drinking glass carried into a room
in the white morning light, drips, ice cold
in a dry hand. Sorrows clear like water
in the glass, the tiny air bubbles
disappear, and the memory is filtered into
the morning light.

Rain that with its light recalls
rain that fell in the past, and voices woven
into it, modulates the frequency
of death, falls briefly,
and has already stopped before the vibrations
become distinct.

A spring morning sweetened by rain, the mild
drizzle that breaks the glazed membrane, it sneaks
a cool thought through your
forehead, strikes a burning spark. Now rain's
fingers have woken up your lips,
swelling without shame.

Suburbs are brought to life by rain, the
dark windows reflect the pale
clearing in the sky, they will just in this moment
open, and the sound of dead voices will come streaming
out, so that the long afternoon of childhood
that did come to an end, might continue in all
its bitter uncertainty.

Washing a liquid balm into the crown
of night, into the seam, into a chamber of
echoes, and to pour on oil, soothe the echo, the comet
and globe, stop the night from falling in
one single operation, reducing pain by reducing
the night, making a crack in the wing-bone
of night.

The sun, too, can bring back a day in May
with a wind that sharpens shadows, takes
a deep breath, whistles around the corners
of the house. Behind the shiny windows are the dead
smiles which take their place again around the
festive table. Whipped cream put out to cool
on the veranda like a too
boisterous child.

Rain comes and digs out the
old courtyard, finds it under the
crumbling asphalt and the high rise. Rain-
light cuts through layers of time,
of ice so that the moon again, after the shower,
will gaze at itself in wet flagstones, in the
painted iron table, the watery remains
of forgotten glasses. Everything in
its place. In the enamelled washbowl the moon
floats like porridge, oatmeal, in milk.

Stick a tube into the night, drain it
of darkness so that the stars become
paler, the distance more distant, and waves
cannot reach the *bone chain* of night, but
become faint distress, a little tension. Subdue
the visions of night with the help of mild violence.

To peck a hole in the night, push it
into ice-cold water, meeting night with
night, controlled, mercifully because the merci-
less action is necessary. Cut into
the red tissue of night and feel how
its galloping pulse slackens.

In the same moment as the last rain-
drop hit the glass (even though the sound
shall continue for all eternity)
the courtyard disappeared, where the tables
were laid with cloths of rain, with glasses, before
anyone had time to run out and gobble down
the watery remains.

To beat the night, not wildly, restrained
so that beating and not beating are expressions
of the same resignation, wait until
you can stand calm and watch your hand
strike, so that night gradually can take part
in the peace you feel.

Cut into night's grand, waving frontal
lobe. Droning night. Isolate a spot
where the skin is thinnest – hypodermis
exposed and glistening – prepare penetration and
discharge.

The hand that doesn't obey, but climbs up
to its own edge, and lets go. It
slides like oil on water, is spawned out,
sluggishly, as if it no longer has a
will. At last it obeys no more,
but is carried.

We become visible there, hanging over the yard
in a reflection brought out by flickering
neon tubes just switched on in a
hot room. We exist there, and no longer
inside, but outside in the hazy air of
the autumn morning.

To run a needle point into night's eye, in
the corner, the star crater, and hit a
barrier. The barrier is the
imagination, sprung out of sacred
uncertainty, the resistance innate in
a hand.

In the pelting rain breaking
up soil – pale bulbs and pieces of
glass shining, crumbling plaster bleeding
white paint – the old garden wall rose
again with an edge of broken glass (under a
forgotten, blackened pergola grapes hung
that were long since drunk,
glistening). The house and garden of
childhood, that fortress of expressive
deafness, was once again and long
enough, the only reality.

What is left of the rain? When we went we left
it behind, thought the place we were in,
the autumn morning, was safe. The clouds that
were reflected in the shiny floor, sailed
away, dropped astern, but above the garage
roof night's white cataract keeps
tearing up the dark.

It rains above the courtyard, but
it does not reach the ground, keeps
circling in the air like a flock of starlings. In
the garden pond lies a black bike
frozen over, weak sunlight breathes on the ice
so that you can catch a glimpse
of wheels among stiffly floating
leaves. Among red currant bushes and their evening
shadows, up the stairs to the veranda
someone is running on high heels, with
a clinking glass, in a small black dress,
confused about what day it
is, what time, for here every day
is a feast.

A beak puncturing night's abdomen or
wings stuck into it so that it must
not crawl on the earth like a
snake. A fire pumped into the texture
of night so that it is lit up from

the inside, even the thinnest veins glow then,
the smallest stars speak their
inhuman language.

To pluck night when it stands tall, bursting
pushing away its shadows, when it is
about to trickle out. Where
flame and night in the end flow together
and freeze. Force the flame down
night's throat, bind the eye of night
to ashes.

Rain that falls in the early hours
when the window is open even though
it is not, smells of salt as
in a wind travelling from afar, and of faint
soap in a naked palm. Rain that comes in
order to leave, tears itself away
so that it can be felt. A light remains
from water that washes over
things and brings out their lost
glow.

To lift night on a stretcher with light's hands,
carry it swinging through dark streets
or drive it in a car, when night

is at its weakest, at daybreak. What strength
it gives! And with this
strength make a wound in the night.

A return to the yellow house with walls
pale from frost, past the comfrey
transparent and grey. Now the child can
walk, in front of you on the bumpy road
with a thin layer of ice, in the cloud of its
own breath, you push the empty pram. Moving
slowly through the woods, over the
silenced river.

To soften night's sorrow with light, scrape
with a laser over the eye just below the
skeleton's arch, cut through to burn
the capillary threads of thought, damage
the roots, so that glad thoughts
can still rise.

To steer night so that it should not be
lost, not by praying or giving way to
tenderness. A bitter mother has the child
in her grip, with bitterness you can bind
the night to you. By exploiting
night you can protect it.

In a while all shall feel easier for
the night. Deadened to the smell
secreted by fear, on the run with half
the brain asleep, there is no longer
a difference between what it loves and should
love. At last it can repent.

Rain sifts unnoticeably through a
narrow opening in time, into this
dry day, casting a shadow over
the garden, over thirsting plants,
silvery grey wooden tables, inside
making dusk descend and a shine drip
from things, from hands and cheeks.
In this rainy darkness all seems
equally insubstantial and threatening.

It rains into the dark kitchen;
here history gathers in a pool
in front of the stove – a cross
section of the drops that fell in bitter summers –
before it disappears between floor
boards, while the fire in the water lights
forward a face dissolved by tenderness.

At last rain fell, bringing with it a
trapdoor, a garden gate on the latch, a
home, in the transition when light
falls softly as it does when
spring arrives. The house stood again for a short
while on the edge of the wood, in
the crossing of the roads or in La Boca (the city's
mouth), shining and trans-
parent, and the voices there were just
about to break the silence
when the rain ceased.

from

Salt on the eye

Vacuum

In the bath when light falls
the murmur from the water dies
the bubbles of lather disappear
remember how big the bar of soap felt in the hand
how the hand strained to hold it?
In the milky water soap fat floated like fish eyes
caught all reflections in the gathering darkness

Passenger

Returning to the car, with an egg-white and red interior,
to steer it not as a driver but as a passenger
On our way through the landscapes of night over bridges on
invisible pylons along a steep coast towards mountain passes, a
floodlit stage. The driver is willing to take the risks involved. I
must keep awake but sleep creeps up on me, alongside the car,
and overtakes me some time in the evening or early morning

Bungalow

It is possible to return to where you have never been
catch sight of a bungalow, almost a shed, on an island
in a river, the spring moon – see how it rides
the river's oily back spreading its dead light
Pay attention when the wind rises at dawn sweeping
the dead-pale moon under the carpet of clouds as it
starts to rain
Hear how thunder drops on the corrugated iron roof (but
distantly) while the flood rises above the threshold
threatening to set afloat this home, a dark nest
Suddenly, perhaps, discover the children in the rowboat
trying with the boathook to get a grip, first on the doorknob,
then the chimney. When the bungalow is pulled under and
lost they cast off, their faces like dimmed glass in the shiny air
above flames

The moon in Loo's house

It clears up towards evening, the road's wet shoulders shine
in the moonlight that pours down and forces its way into the
house where Loo's mother wades on a well-trodden carpet path
(visible from the moon) between the kitchen and the lounge.
She juggles with titbits, tumblers and elastic smiles, which she
practices in front of the mirror all day, with mewing sounds.
Jack Daniels and slim Johnny Walker have come to supper,
they get a golden glow from the moon that resembles a lemon
slice in the bottom of the tumbler. Loo's father's pale moonlit-
hand beckons us. We must greet his pals, put our arms around
their necks and kiss them, although we are afraid. He flings his
hand out so the bottles dance on the table reflected in the TV-
screen where pictures from the moon landing roll, the great
step for mankind this night in July. As the flies sail on waves of
moonlight in the clammy room, ether produces images of the
earth from afar. It seems almost impossible to distinguish which
heavenly body, earth or moon, is the more distant

The admirer

I flee into the bathroom
shut behind me the pale-grey door
with its glass of irregular drops
unaware that someone is already there
(or did she manage to sneak in?)
until I glance in the mirror and see
a figure sitting half hidden behind the laundry basket
in tights that are too long
the feet tied together
While I think of what to say she speaks:
"You must forgive me I don't want to impose
but I must make myself known to you once in a while
to feel that I am real"
She tries to get up
"a need that you evidently don't share"
she adds as she falls forward

Terri's house

It is possible to return to Terri's house. The cemetery is
probably still there right opposite on a small hill. The house
blinks its windows in the afternoon heat and the garage gapes
over a darkness larger than itself with a musty smell. The wire
door to the house screeches as it closes. It takes a while before
my eyes can see us sitting there in the lounge on the sofa with
legs glued together. I enter the uncomfortable shadow of
my small body, each finger a thumb and my mouth a trunk,
I suck up the powdered milk served in blue glasses by Terri's
mother (she seems like her grandmother even though I know
that they cut corners in their time). My eyes water, sweat
runs down my back, like last time, the sofa's polythene cover
is sticky with deep scars. In the burning silence I can hear
the moth hearts of our shadows mixed in with the buzzing
of flies behind the terry cloth curtains. A kind of devotional
atmosphere spreads, the clock on the wall strikes heavily, our
midriffs swing, the glasses chime on the coffee table. Terri has
the quietest shadow, it bows and thanks us for coming. I stare
at the wrinkly hands entangled on her lap, the silvery stripes
in her soft childish hair, when she slowly lifts her shadow head
she catches me red handed again. Now with hindsight I can tell
her gaze is bashful and hostile, but I still cannot fathom why
her smile begs to be slapped

Halloween

The darkest most receptive time of year forms a tract
of silence and dead voices in a strange buzz of echoes
But it is possible to distinguish the slight weeping that rises
from a festive photo, make contact with the restlessness that
can break open or bang shut
It is time to peep into the living room where the picture was
taken, dare to enter, walk around on the flossy carpet
with a crunching sound in the layers of crumbs
and insects, leaving no tracks
take a deep breath, cleanse the nostrils with the smell of
pungent dust
pull your hand over the damp back of a chair with
protruding shoulder blades
try the false piano (with fingers stiff from fear the way
you always played, the music unattainable, it never came to
your rescue)
time to throw a glance at the coffee table with shades
of spots from thirst-quenching drinks, the white rings
under a film of fatty polish
and dare to gaze at the five figures on the sofa, and be terrified
by a ghost, two vampire princesses, a pirate
and a small unhappy goblin

"That the juices may flow in them/
And the juices lie."

He spoke of the pearls that followed the dancer's motions back and forth, crowding in waves that rushed after her over the marble floor in the centre courtyard, like glazed grains of salt on a solidly frozen lake in the field of her inconstant shadow. "Then she stopped" he said, and it was impossible to read from his face if he was making it up or telling the truth, but what is the difference? "Her dark blue skirt waved and sparkled for there is always some sand in the wind there, like moon dust" he added. "A wisp of hair stuck to her pale lips, she looked straight ahead towards the darkness behind the columns, her gaze introverted. She remained like this, standing with her legs planted apart, lifting her arms while the fingers ignited the stars in the night sky, and one by one the pearls started to float. Gathered into a small cloud, they began to rise up her legs under her skirt." He wanted to turn away but couldn't move his eyes, controlled by something other than will. How long she held the pearls inside her before she let go he had no idea, but when the cascade hit the floor it felt as though he had wept

Transfer

I meet her on the train that cool May night a short
moment when silence seeps through
notice the oversized clip in her
thin hair the surprisingly shiny polythene coat
her face pale as salt when she steps off the train
sends me a smile beyond reach
reminds me of the phone that rings when I am about to
sleep, it goes on ringing and ringing but then stops

Haunted

Is it her? In the corridor I am struck by doubt
Fancy I should meet her here so unexpectedly on the
street in a strange city. I pretend to be happy
truthfulness has never been my strongest trait
but now it's too late, I have invited her in. As if to
limit the madness I confess we are living here now
but only for a while
Please, I offer her a glass of wine
What should I do otherwise?
Suddenly she kneels down before me, a white light
runs down her back in a broad band from
the wrung shoulder, gathering on her soles
Does the light come from her sun-warm head?
Or does my gaze try to eliminate her?

Soundtrack

Like a butterfly in strong wind consciousness moves
through dream in waking
is pushed from room to room pulling suddenly through
floors ceilings walls
becomes shadows of walls
dictated by the uncertain flapping
From a distant courtyard that could (not) have been different
well known sounds rise hushing falsetto confessions
distorted crying the rattling of knives and forks
silvery dark clangs of ice-
cubes
The sound track follows the flight even as the room drowns
consciousness reaches light and some stability

from Desert conditions

I came to the fields and spacious palaces
of the desert, breathed out, caught a glimpse of many things I
thought had been lost
"my" first piano (wobbling on the sand), a black basin with its
whirling eye intact
tulips from childhood with their sharp shadows, a red
stool I had only read of but made mine (half
buried)
and a sandy bar of soap dissolved
long ago

On the line stretched between two peaks the caftan waves
in the desert wind, like frost in a beard or fur
the sand sticks to its folds the wind
and a blizzard of sand
penetrates the wool until it becomes so heavy the
mountains cave in

Buried in the sand so that only the eyes are visible
those on the shell like pinioned hands
the creature keeps rolling these eyes, tries to
blink the sand away
through the cataracts a juice is pumped out
that should clear salt away keep the gaze pure
so it can mirror light from the stars but
the image is floating in a sheen of pain

The sand's skeleton melts, rises towards the surface
stretches, dissolves slowly before it becomes visible
because the sand swells, the passage narrows
in the heat
When the conch of sand gives off cries (in the soundless
registers) vibrations start, the vibrating membrane
of the sand's crust turns clear but not transparent

Vehement wind takes hold of the sand, has its own ears
to hear with, locked in its organ peal (*Wachet auf ruft
uns die Stimme*) or in its flight engine that races
In the cockpit of sand it is quiet, when you put your ear
to the rippling dunes you can feel a pressure at high
or low frequency as a trembling or loss of heat

Rain warmer than tears slightly warmer than skin pours
over this landscape so the sky lights up
shiny *hamadas* (naked rock)
among towers of supposedly untouched sand but the sand
sweats
salt bleeds in dried out river beds, pools and
suddenly the rain seems cool

Silence shall come move the air breathe on a dark
double-sided mirror
float too high and too
low over the sand and still penetrate it, fill the
ventricles the way wells in the earth are filled
but break into sound when the temperature rises

In the dark

The spring sun dug out remains of a meal in the flower bed
chicken bones pale fringe roots with a
thin layer of humus a narrow skull with a gaping beak
soil-filled eye hollows (the size of a flower bulb)
a bent fork a bottle that craned its neck
The remnants sparkled like treasure in the wet ground
Was it once a meal in praise of spring? Did they serve
the bird with its head? Drink cheap wine? Too much?
The sun is about to give up and leave the garden
in the inner court
Even though light is in the sky
darkness takes over here below, replaces all questions
with calm

Visible and invisible

Like shadows in spring sharp yet transparent
the faces of people pass on the ramparts by the river (the wind
rubs shiny wounds on the surface)
Winter has worn them as salt can corrode the eye
spring air drains them so their bones are more visible
in matted cheeks
They walk bare-headed along the white blurred walls
their hair-roots suck up sun which flows over the skull
runs along their stiff spines like warm oil
I read on the pale lips that soon everything may
explode

The bathtub's history

The small lion's feet sink further and further into the ground
every spring when the frost leaves so that the belly of the
apricot-coloured bathtub brushes the lawn
It floats on a cargo of dead leaves (and things that have
happened here that I still don't believe to be true)
on steady course for a new flowering. But soon
in a few hundred years, the tub will travel under ground and
neither grass nor wind shall betray it

The limitless

I meet her on the beach in early spring
one of those days that flows over with too much light
the tarpaulins flap this cold morning
She emerges suddenly between the boat cradles
much smaller than I remember, I gape in surprise
hear the plastic smacking around us the wind whistling
in my mouth. "Don't hang your head!" she cries and comes
towards me sideways like a crab, and I cannot see
her expression which avoids the light but know she will
smile when she turns
And since I
so often have defied commands of the heart, eaten
feeling nauseated swallowed my words signalled with
my fingers instead of asking, I will return the smile

Purification

I turned on the taps, the sound of gushing water turned
into a droning as if the tub was a clock, the jet hit the
natural frequency
Lay back in the chiming waves (only my hair visible)
the rim and the sides felt like an egg
not the hard shell but hardboiled white
I cut off the water
In the silence expectation quivered, I sweated more when
the heat disappeared
steam and the cloth I rubbed myself with smelled of salt

Primitive

What we buried were small liquor bottles (from swimming pools
and glove compartments) grey-pink soaps with dark
scars
having spent a long time on the sink in wet surroundings
they had still dried up
a little red make-up (from a stranger's purse)
red doll's hair but I don't know why we wanted
to shave the doll with long legs
and a pile of pictures we had collected from black and
white magazines we found under a bed
Crammed it all together in a jam jar that we lay in
a shallow hole in the cemetery on a windy day
(if hands are small and the spade large two can do better)
A picture floating in the air above this distant place
springs from light waves time has broken
and magnifies what we did
what we were able to rescue

Knife in the water

Her body smiles at him under water
a glinting knife under the surface with tiny ripples
The morning sun has loosened her from the sheath
expands her
she becomes heavy and rushes into him

Loo's memory

With intensified strength the memory of Loo shines
A lot about her reminded me of grass
her soft fingers her smile thin hair
the crooked waistband tight over her stomach
like a sheaf – her skirt cut short above her aching knees
(because this suited a girl best)
She rises out of an ice-cold pool or
slips away in the back seat of a car
her head bigger than I remember but still small
(a small ball in the grass)
Her voice with a rush the way straws can sound
is not dead

Real and unreal light

The water in the basin suddenly flares up
the cheek of the child just in from the cold
plays in blue hues
And long after darkness has drunk all colours
the child's eye which I saw against the sun
continues to glow

A white spot

Dive into memory and come to
an unrecognizable place
though I must have been here before
Flying in over a small town with straight streets
small houses in rows
it is snowing but that's unusual since all cars are parked
The place seems desolate
Maybe evening is on its way
What is the latitude?
The sun has been erased from the sky but how far
has it sunk below the horizon
what lines have I crossed
Sailing on wings of snow closing my eyes
I feel it lashes wet against my face
About to land I open my eyes
stirring up much snow I find myself standing by
a newly dug grave
with soil steaming in the cold
Suddenly encircled by a tiny flock
of mourners in black
I must after all have been here a while
for my thinly dressed legs have frozen to sticks
and my cheeks are stiff from tears
I feel the blood rising
Who lies in the coffin?
How can I have forgotten this?
Someone breathes warm against my neck
holding my shoulders with a stranger's grip
There is only the snow to hold on to

Exposure

In the opening between two straight lines that
intersect in the water she surges in front of him
he bends forward thinks his shadow
can cover the angle where her naked body
shines in the sun and hide her completely
but in the tension
(when the eye too secretes salt)
a dislocation always takes place

Passage

Where is she? I peek into living room (where morning
takes a nap to the sound of pots and pans, a buzz
from the radio before the sun pierces its neck) Wandering
down the corridor through many swinging doors, maybe
she has just passed by here? The building is so silent but
something flaps near my ear. The snowy weather which
started carefully has become grey flames around pockets
in the air. Can anything throw a shadow in
such chaos? The skin is transparent in winter with
red specks (from calyxes of the blood)
because the heart beats faster in the cold. Is this true?
I stopped by the chapel, the face of the one lying there
was completely transformed

Florence revisited

The road to Florence was not as I
remember, did not melt in the sun so that I
had to row the last part of the way out to the sea
She did not meet me on the pier where a thousand
crabs hurried so it sounded like thunder
Lightning was not reflected in wet crab shells
or heavily waving sails, for I don't know
whether it rained this November afternoon
or whether it was salt spray that
dimmed the windows in the clam chowder cafe
I could have sworn it stood on piles
in the sea that rushed and thumped under the boards
and that the steam from the soup pans
and the wine breath of the guests
trickled on the pane
I see her face behind the dim glass
as if I stood outside looking in
but at the same time sat opposite her by
the white-dressed table, slightly irritated
by the way she stuffed the spoon in her mouth
pouted her lips, her voice drowned
Now it is more distinct, flies into the room
where the cafe still stands she still sits
while I enter the bus with crabs in a bag
take the shortest route back across the ocean

She has gone before

I

Even so I sometimes walk beside her
or a bit in front or a bit behind
through a blue hall out into a Formica kitchen
with a counter and sky-high stools where
the floor (all glossy surfaces) shines comfortingly
the room is still with devotion. We come tiptoeing
She presses her blunt child's finger to her lips
looks around as if about to avert a flood
while she totters on aching knees
I notice then how her flanneled chest
vibrates in slow motion. In the same instant as
the day appears and warm beams strike us
in this room scrubbed after a feast
something jerks under the night gown fabric
Her heart pecks (a bird wanting out)
I can still feel her hand growing numb
when she seizes mine

II

Even so I still look her up
go and stand beside her
in the hall with walls that radiate a blue heat
when the darkness of a feast descends and remnants of
daylight flash in puddles from the snow the guests dragged in
but they dry up quickly
I can make out the rabbit teeth under her lip
detect a whistling as she breathes
even though I know she tries so hard to check herself
The daughters of this tribe can keep a secret

the way others keep their food down
We stand among damp coats and furs
with our faces snuggled into a stranger's Persian lamb
the lids fastened tightly round the light from our eyes
so that it shall not spill

III

Even so I walk back to find her
in a hurry or I might miss her
if she is standing somewhere along the route
I must make haste before she falls asleep
in the apartment block by the edge of the wood
I should have been there long ago
Spring is on its way with feverish nights, sharp stars
the snow crust crushes with each staccato breath
It's been a long time since autumn when winds came in
swinging diagonally over the fjord and a younger city
Even though the house stood firm I should have been there
The light from the reading lamp made the surfaces in the circle
shine dimly but something must
have influenced her eyes and diffused everything?
She lay the book aside and mounted her bed
as the floor started slanting and dissolved
To focus she shook her head
She descended into night's tunnel where the wind is stilled
to be taken through stone and dream to light
and there things shall overlap the forms of things
without the blurred edges

Imprisoned

One day in winter I passed by a tree
Now when the sun scorches the hillsides
and light again overflows
it already seems long ago
When I approached the tree
I thought I saw two white angels
caught in the snow covered crown
their wings entangled in the branches
Trembling so that feathers sifted down
they tried to huddle together
I carefully shook the tree
pushed against the trunk
and when the snow slid I saw
how red and shiny their feet were
their cloaks flecked with ashes
as if an accident had occured
That is why they had landed
in this part of the spectrum
where the radiance can influence sight

Preserved

We wanted to bury the lie
Like tulips on cold spring days
it thrived well enough in the light
to make a new appearance

Took all the letters we found and put them in a jar
with boiling sea water
The salt sealed the writing but
made it less distinct

Creatures

We spent the day on the beach with no hope that anything
should happen but a prayer that nothing would
Swam in the grey weather sat and read with our feet in
the sand that still held some warmth
Her thin pigtail just covered the eye on her neck
and rubbed against her poplin back
O that squeaking sound! A tone of survival in the storm
When she bent forward to get up
and go down to the water her eye searching
no one was there to see her except me
and it is not like the moon
footprints will not be left for millions of years

Notes

p.11 From the letters of Rosa Luxemburg as quoted in Jane Cooper's poem 'Threads: Rosa Luxemburg from Prison' in *Scaffolding*, 1984.

p.21 Muriel Rukeyser, 'The Outer Banks', *The Speed of Darkness*, 1968.

p.23 From the notes of Thomas Hariot quoted at an exhibition about Sir Walter Ralegh's Roanoke, The British Museum, 1985.

p.24 Charles Baudelaire, 'La Musique', *Les Fleurs du mal*, 1857.

p.28 "The true twentieth century" is Anna Akhmatova's expression.

p.32 Carl von Linné, *Ölandska resa* (Travel to Öland), 1741.

p.34 Novalis, 'Lied des Einsiedlers'.

p.35 Lorine Niedecker, 'Paean to Place', *My Life by Water, Collected Poems*, 1968.

p.37 Muriel Rukeyser, 'The Gates', *The Gates*, 1976

p.38 Robert Duncan, 'Answering', *Roots and Branches*, 1964.

p.45 Ferhad Shakely, 'Qamishly'.

p.101 "That the juices may flow in them/ And the juices lie." is from George Oppen's poem 'A Language of New York' in *This in Which*, 1965.

p.105 Saint Augustine, *Confessions*, X, 8 (Pusey's translation as quoted in Frances A. Yates, *The Art of Memory*.)

p.120 Florence here is Florence, Oregon, USA.

Hanne Bramness is a Norwegian poet, editor, translator, and novelist. Born in 1959, she published her first Norwegian collection *Korrespondanse* in 1983 and has followed this with seven other collections, two of them – *Kysset* and *Trollmåne* – for children. Her other collections are *I sin tid* (1986), *Nattens kontinent* (1992), *Revolusjonselegier* (1996), *Regnet i Buenos Aires* (2002) and *Salt på øyet* (2006). She won the Norwegian Poetry Club Prize in 1996 and the prestigious Dobloug Prize from the Swedish Academy in 2006.

Hanne Bramness' many translations include works by Mina Loy, Kamala Das, Denise Levertov and William Blake. She lives in Oslo.

www.ingramcontent.com/pod-product-compliance
Lightning Source LLC
Chambersburg PA
CBHW031154160426
43193CB00008B/360